JULIANA'S BANANAS

Where do your bananas come from?

WRITTEN AND ILLUSTRATED
BY RUTH WALTON

With many thanks to the K. Blundell Trust, the Windward Islands Farmers' Association, Liz Parker, Renwick and Ancelma Rose, Philemon Allen, Amos Wiltshire, Sylma Cornelius, Eddma Wiltshire, Errol and Marcella Harris, Simon Leon, Moses Rene, Jacqui Mackay, Banana Link, Joe Venables, Nicholas Faisal, The Fairtrade Foundation – and Juliana Wiltshire, who inspired the fictional character in this story.

CONTENTS

Bertha and her brother Billy live in the Windward Islands. They live in a blue house with their mother Juliana. Lots of fruit and vegetables grow in their garden. What can you see growing?

MANGO

SUGAR CANE

COCONUT

YAM

BANANA

SWEET POTATO

THE WINDWARD ISLANDS

WHERE ARE THE WINDWARD ISLANDS?

SOUTH AMERICA

AFRICA

CARIBBEAN SEA

DOMINICA

MARTINIQUE

SAINT LUCIA

SAINT VINCENT AND THE GRENADINES

GRENADA

The Windward Islands are in the West Indies, on the eastern side of the Caribbean Sea. All of the islands are countries except Martinique, which is part of France!

5

Every day, Juliana works in the garden growing bananas to sell. Bananas grow all year round, so there is fruit to pick every week. Sometimes, Billy and Bertha play between the banana plants. Can you see something they have left behind?

SUCKER

BANANA FLOWER

GROWING BANANAS

The small banana plant is called a sucker. When the plant is around six months old it grows a large red flower. After this flower opens, the bananas start to grow in a big bunch.

Juliana puts a bag over the bananas
to protect them from insects and birds.

The banana plant is not a tree — it's actually the world's largest herb!

The banana plant has two different kinds of flower! Inside the large red flower, each tiny banana has a small white flower on the end of it.

7

When Juliana goes to work, Bertha and Billy catch the bus to school.

The journey is quick in the school bus and it picks up lots more children on the way.

At school Bertha and Billy meet their friends Marsha and Errol.

Before the lessons start, they play together in the school yard.

Bertha's favourite lesson is science. The school has lots of exciting equipment to make learning fun!

Bertha and Marsha play with a model of the planets to learn how the solar system works.

HOW MANY PLANETS CAN YOU SEE?

Billy and Errol are in the computer room, working on the school newsletter.

There is some important news for all the children's parents. The weather forecast is very bad and a hurricane is coming!

That night, the hurricane comes. The wind is strong and lightning fills the sky. Juliana has nailed boards over the windows to help the family stay safe.

The electricity is cut off and the family must stay inside until the storm is over. Inside the house Billy and Bertha can't sleep because the wind is so loud. Juliana reads them a story by torch light.

It's important to have some bottled drinking water in a hurricane because water pipes are often broken by the storm!

This battery-powered radio will help the family keep up to date with island news while there is no electricity.

When morning comes, the banana plants have blown over in the wind.

Juliana is very upset and angry. All of her hard work has been undone.

Juliana works hard to clear the field and grow another crop of bananas. It will take nine months before the new crop is ready.

AMAZING FACTS

WHAT IS A HURRICANE?

A hurricane is a large circular tropical storm with heavy rain and strong winds. Hurricanes start over warm oceans and the winds blow in a spiral shape. This picture shows what a hurricane looks like from above.

Hurricane season in the Caribbean is from June until November, but climate change has meant that the storms can strike at any time. Each hurricane is given a name. The first storm of the year has a name starting with A, the second storm's name will start with B, until the whole alphabet is used. If a storm is very bad its name will never be used again.

HURRICANE POWER!

Hurricane Tomas hit the Windward Islands in October 2010. In Saint Lucia and Saint Vincent nearly every banana tree was destroyed. The winds were up to 100 miles (160 kilometres) an hour. Millions of dollars worth of damage was caused.

DID YOU KNOW...?

In other parts of the world hurricanes can be called cyclones or typhoons.

The new banana plants are nearly fully grown, but big black spots start to appear on the leaves.

The plants are sick and Juliana will have to work hard to help them get better.

The mango tree is full of fruit. Billy and Bertha climb the tree to help pick the mangoes.

Juliana collects them in a basket to sell at the market.

AMAZING FACTS

PLANTS CAN GET ILL TOO...

Black Sigatoka is a disease that affects banana plants. It makes their leaves turn black and yellow and stops them from making as many bananas.

The disease is hard to cure and farmers have to buy expensive treatments for the plants. If a banana plant is very ill, it is cut down.

WHAT DO BANANAS AND DINOSAURS HAVE IN COMMON?

Bananas may become extinct, just like the dinosaurs! Until the 1950s, most bananas sold and eaten were of a variety called Gros Michel. By 1960 this variety was completely wiped out by a banana illness called Panama disease.

The type of banana that is most common today is called the Cavendish. Experts predict that Cavendish bananas could become extinct within the next 30 years too!

The banana plants are finally growing well. Once a week, Juliana pays people to come and help pick the fruit. Bertha and Billy have come to watch the harvest. The whole bunch is cut while it is still green, using a big knife called a cutlass. After the bananas have been cut, the plant is chopped down and a new sucker will grow in its place.

The bananas are taken to the packing shed. Juliana cuts them into smaller bunches, washes them and packs them into cardboard boxes.

The boxes are loaded onto the back of a truck. Bertha and Billy watch them drive away and wonder where they are going...

The truck takes the bananas to the port. The boxes are weighed and checked for quality. They are packed into a huge metal box called a shipping container. Once a week, a big ship calls at the port to collect the bananas. The container is loaded onto the ship using a crane.

The Renwick Rose

As the boat travels through the Windward Islands collecting bananas, it also delivers lots of other goods. Everything that isn't made on the islands has to be shipped in, including dried foods, steel, diggers, farm machinery, car parts, condensed milk and even fire engines!

19

HOW DO BANANAS TURN YELLOW?

Bananas turn yellow when they are ripe. To ripen they need to be warm. When the bananas arrive at their destination they are taken to a ripening centre.

The bananas are put into warm rooms which are filled with a natural gas called ethylene that helps the bananas ripen and turn yellow.

The bananas are carefully checked to make sure they are the perfect shade of yellow! When they are just right, they are packed into trucks and taken to the supermarket to be sold.

DID YOU KNOW...?

Bananas get sweeter as they turn from green to yellow and brown.

The bananas are ready to buy! It has taken around two weeks for the fruit to travel from Juliana's farm to the supermarket shelves. Rachel, Eva and Harry are out shopping and buy a bunch of Fairtrade bananas.

When they get home,
Rachel, Harry and Eva make
some delicious banana and
almond smoothies to drink.

FIND THESE YUMMY BANANA RECIPES ON PAGES 24–25

Juliana, Bertha and Billy are eating. Today they are having banana fritters for dessert and drinking mango juice.

FACT FILE

In the Windward Islands, green bananas are called figs and they are often cooked in savoury dishes. The national dish of Saint Lucia is 'green fig and salt fish' and it is often eaten for breakfast!

FAIRTRADE BANANA RECIPES

You can try making Rachel and Juliana's tasty banana recipes too! Make sure you have got an adult to help you in the kitchen.

BANANA & ALMOND SMOOTHIE

INSTRUCTIONS: Put the oats and seeds into a blender and whizz until they have turned to powder. Add the peeled bananas, almond milk and date syrup or honey and blend until everything is smooth and creamy.

INGREDIENTS:
2 tbsp rolled oats
2 tbsp mixed seeds
2 Fairtrade bananas
2 cups / 500ml almond milk
If you can't get almond milk, you can use any other kind of milk!
1 tbsp date syrup or honey

EXPERIMENT! Try adding different ingredients to your smoothie – how about a handful of mixed berries, a spoonful of yoghurt or a ripe avocado?

BANANA FRITTERS

These fritters work best with very ripe bananas. If the peel is brown, the fritters will be even more tasty! This recipe makes around 12 small fritters.

INSTRUCTIONS:

1. Peel the bananas and put them into a mixing bowl. Mash them with a fork until they are thick and gooey.

2. Sift the flour into the bowl, then add the other ingredients and stir them with a wooden spoon until they are well mixed.

INGREDIENTS:

3 very ripe Fairtrade bananas
½ cup / 80g plain all-purpose flour
½ tsp baking powder
2 tbsp sugar
½ tsp vanilla essence
½ tsp cinnamon
¼ tsp grated nutmeg
¼ cup / 60ml water
1 tbsp lemon juice
2 tbsp coconut oil for frying

If you can't get coconut oil, you can use vegetable oil. Remember you can also buy Fairtrade sugar, vanilla, cinnamon, nutmeg and lemons!

3. Get an adult to heat the coconut oil in a heavy pan. Add tablespoon-sized blobs of batter to the pan. Cook the fritters on a medium heat for 2 or 3 minutes on each side, until they are crisp and brown.

4. Place on a paper towel before serving to soak up any extra grease.

For a special treat, serve with maple syrup or cinnamon sugar...

WHY BUY FAIRTRADE BANANAS?

When your family buys bananas, look out for the FAIRTRADE Mark. When farmers sell Fairtrade bananas, they get a fair price and extra money to spend on their farms or in their communities. This is called the Fairtrade Premium. Here are some of the things that the Fairtrade Premium has paid for in the Windward Islands...

This school in Saint Lucia has lots of computers to help children learn to read and type.

This school in Saint Vincent has a science laboratory filled with exciting equipment.

The grass on this football field in Dominica is kept short with a lawn mower that was paid for with the Fairtrade Premium, so for the first time children like Billy and Bertha have somewhere safe to play football after school.

This school bus travels around the island of Saint Vincent twice a day, helping lots of children from the countryside get to school and back safely!

BANANA WORKERS WORLDWIDE

Not all banana workers work on small farms like Juliana's. Many of them work on plantations owned by big companies. Life for all banana workers can be very difficult – but those producing Fairtrade bananas are protected from the most harmful conditions.

Some companies spray chemicals onto banana plants from planes, which can pollute the environment and can make their workers very ill. Fairtrade banana farms cannot use the most dangerous chemicals.

On Fairtrade banana farms, workers are always given protective clothing to wear when they are using chemicals.

Workers on Fairtrade banana farms wear gloves when they wash fruit. This stops their hands becoming sore and helps to protect them from getting stomach upsets.

In the Windward Islands, the extra money from selling Fairtrade bananas has helped lots of farmers like Juliana to treat diseased plants and repair the damage caused by hurricanes.

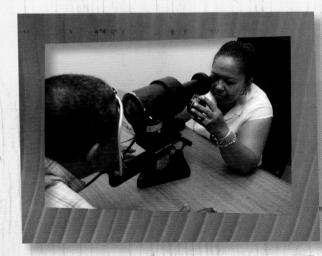

The Fairtrade Premium has helped to pay for lots of good things for farmers and their communities around the world, like this eye clinic in the Dominican Republic.

MEET SOME REAL LIFE BANANA WORKERS

Rohan works at the docks in Saint Vincent. He makes sure the bananas are top quality before they are loaded into the ship.

Amos and Sylma grow bananas in Dominica. Amos spends all day at the farm working hard to keep the banana plants healthy and free from weeds.

Nelson works at the port in Saint Vincent. He makes sure the bananas are loaded onto the ship quickly and safely.

Lee works at a ripening centre in the UK. He makes sure the bananas are ripe and ready to be eaten.

Erika works at a ripening centre in the UK. She checks the bananas before they leave for the supermarket.

It's the end of the day in the Windward Islands and Billy and Bertha are tired. Juliana is looking forward to a good night's sleep after a long day growing bananas!